Our Father

Books by William C. Mills

Pastoral Ministry

*Church, World, and Kingdom: The Eucharistic Foundations
of Alexander Schmemann's Pastoral Theology*

Kyprian Kern: Orthodox Pastoral Service

*Called to Serve: Readings on Ministry From the Orthodox
Church*

Church and World: Essays in Honor of Michael Plekon

Biblical Prayer and Spirituality

A 30 Day Retreat: A Personal Guide to Spiritual Renewal

Walking with God: Stories of Life and Faith

Come Follow Me

The Prayer of St. Ephrem: A Biblical Commentary

Our Father: A Prayer for Christian Living

Encountering Jesus in the Gospels

Lectionary Series

A Light to the Gentiles: Reflections on the Gospel of Luke

*Baptize All Nations: Reflections on the Gospel of Matthew
for the Pentecostal Season*

Feasts of Faith: Reflections on the Major Feast Days

From Pascha to Pentecost: Reflections on the Gospel of John

*Let Us Attend: Reflections on the Gospel of Mark for the
Lenten Season*

*Prepare O Bethlehem: Reflections on the Scripture Readings
for the Christmas-Epiphany Season*

OUR FATHER

A Prayer for Christian Living

William C. Mills

First Published by Orthodox Research Institute, 2008
Reprinted by OCABS Press, 2018

ISBN 1-60191-046-0 (Paperback)

For

My Parishioners

With

Thanksgiving and Love

TABLE OF CONTENTS

INTRODUCTION

I am always amazed at the large number of spiritu- ality books that are published every year; books on prayer, fasting, pilgrimage, stewardship, Scripture study, and so forth. Every month new books on the Christian spiritual tradition are available for pur- chase. However, the media reports that atheism is on the rise, that people no longer believe in God, and that Church services are irrelevant. In this present time of spiritual ferment and transition in our culture, at least a few people are going through some deep soul searching. Many people are still attending Church and are going back to the basics, especially regarding Christian spirituality. At least we know some of them are also reading books on Christian spirituality!

This should tell us that something important is taking place. First and foremost it means that a lot of Americans are looking for spirituality that is life-giv- ing and will keep them going for the long term. They want substance not pleasant platitudes. They are tired of televangelists who preach a prosperity gospel and seven simple ways to be happy and healthy. People are seeking spiritual practices that engage both head and heart and that provide both breadth and depth. In other words, they want to live faithfully in this world, engaging the culture around them, as the rock star Bono from the rock group U2 once sang, "I still haven't found what I'm looking for," and most people have not found what they are looking for — yet thankfully they are still looking.

Of all the spiritual practices, prayer seems to be number one on their list. When people are down and out, they pray. When people mourn the death of a loved one, they pray. When people are discouraged, they pray. When they are suffering, they pray.

Even though prayer is important, many people do not know how to pray. Very often people ask me about prayer. I usually turn to the Lord's Prayer, since of all the prayers in the Christian tradition, the Lord's Prayer is the only one from Jesus Himself. That is quite amazing, that for 2,000 years we have been reciting and singing the same words that Jesus taught His disciples.

The Lord's Prayer, which is also often referred to as the, "Our Father," is only a few short verses, but within these verses the entire Christian life is given to us. People pray or sing the Lord's Prayer without paying much attention to the words that they are saying. We recite the Lord's Prayer at home before meals; we say it throughout the day; we say it at Church, but do we know what the prayer means? Do we know what it means when we say that God's name is "hallowed"? Or what it means to ask God to give us our "daily bread"? I am sure that when my daughters pray this petition they are probably thinking about divine peanut butter and jelly sandwiches, but Jesus has something else in mind.

People want to learn more about the Lord's Prayer. They want to know the meaning of these ancient and arcane words. Furthermore, many people are surprised that we have not just one, but two versions of the Lord's Prayer, one in the Gospel of Matthew and the other in Luke! They are also amazed that even though there are hundreds of Christian denominations that are separated by time, space, and theology, the one prayer that unites all of us under the authority and command of God is the Lord's Prayer. When we pray the Lord's Prayer, we are uniting ourselves to one another in a common voice, sharing our faith with one another. This prayer brings people together in a bond of love and solidarity.

THE LORD'S PRAYER AND DISCIPLESHIP. In seven short verses, the Lord's Prayer lays out for us the Christian way of discipleship. This is also the narrow way and the way of the cross. But it is a way for all of us since Jesus invites every one of us to follow. Jesus called Peter, James, John, and Andrew,

who were fisherman, just as He called Matthew the
tax collector, Philip and Nathaniel and the other disciples too. Jesus also calls us with the same invitation
in which He called the first disciples, to "come and
follow Me." Sure this sounds easy, and Jesus even said
it was, "My burden is easy and my yoke is light." Jesus
calls us, but do we always follow? Well, sometimes we
do and sometimes we don't, usually our own pride,
programs, and agendas get in the way of following
Him. Yet God still calls out "come and follow Me."

The Lord's Prayer is important for discipleship.
The word disciple means student and the earliest disciples were students of Jesus. Jesus taught them just as
any teacher would teach their students. Jesus taught
His disciples a lot of things. He taught them about
fasting, prayer, almsgiving, evangelism, performing
works of mercy and having a spirit of commitment
and obedience. He also taught them about rest and
relaxation, following the notion of the Sabbath rest,
which is just as important as His other teachings. If
the disciples didn't take time for rest, they would not
be ready to go and preach the Gospel to all nations.

Jesus' teachings are found in the four Gospels,
Matthew, Mark, Luke, and John. If the early Christians had colleges and universities, I think that the
Gospel of Matthew would be used as a textbook because it contains so many of Jesus' teachings on the
spiritual life. The Gospel of Matthew is an outline
of what the Christian community is supposed to be

like, and this community is very practical, pastoral, and ethical. Faith in Jesus does not only require our head but our heart and our hands too! His disciples are called to believe in Him, but this belief also requires action. The disciples acted upon their faith in the Lord.

Furthermore, Jesus did not describe this new life in vague abstractions or generalizations, He spoke directly to the people. When Jesus taught about forgiveness, He didn't say, "Well, I suggest that if you want to be nice that you forgive other people." No, He said, "Forgive others as your heavenly Father has forgiven you." Forgiveness is not an option, but a command. Jesus didn't say, "if you fast" or "if you pray," but "when you fast" and "when you pray." In other words, Jesus expects that we will be forgiving other people, even our enemies! I find this one to be a hard teaching, how can I love my enemy, the one who I hate, get angry at, and even despise. If forgiveness is important to Jesus, it should be important to me.

Another word that pops up now and then in the Gospels, and is very important for discipleship, is the word servant or slave, a term that Jesus uses to refer to Himself such as in the following statement from the Gospel of Mark, "the greatest of all is the one who serves." Slaves were common in the Roman Empire. There were slaves that worked in the kitchen, others worked in the farms and vineyards, and others who instructed their master's children.

Yet Jesus refers to Himself as a servant. Towards the end of His life, just after His last supper with His disciples and just prior to His arrest and trial in Jerusalem, Jesus washed His disciples feet and said that those who want to be His disciples will wash one another's feet. Jesus is speaking to us, if we want to be His disciples we also have to be servants as well. Washing stinky dirty feet does not sound so exciting, yet Jesus commands us that it is through service and humility that we become His disciples.

Being disciples and servants of Jesus means that we have an important task. We actually have to live according to what we pray in Church. The conclusion of our Sunday is not the end of our work but rather it is the beginning. On Sunday, our priest sends us out to do works of mercy, to visit the sick, and to comfort the afflicted and those who are in pain. We are sent out to visit the prisoners and shut-ins, to bring the healing hand of Christ to the world. We are sent out to feed the hungry and help the homeless and the hopeless. Sunday worship informs and shapes our life so that we can actually go out and do good works. So as we pray and sing hymns during the liturgical services, we should use those as guides for our life, so that when we pray for the poor we should be reminded to help the poor. When we hear about peace, we should leave the service and try to become peacemaker to those around us. When we hear about unity, we should leave and become ambassadors of unity in this world. When we receive Jesus' broken body and spilled blood in the Eucharist, we turn and share this brokenness with the world around us which helps heal the world.

The Lord's Prayer is the Christian mission statement to the world. A mission statement is usually a brief one-page summary about the primary aim of an institution or business. For example, when you go to a fast food restaurant, the mission statement might read, "We aim to serve you a hot meal according to the best standards in the industry in the shortest time" and then it may continue for a few more sentences describing the quality of the food and of the company. The mission statement for a large medical facility might read, "Our mission is to provide timely health care to our patients in a responsible manner." The Christian mission statement is the Lord's Prayer. The more that we pray and study the Lord's prayer, hopefully the more committed we will be to Christ and the Church. It isn't always easy, but yet we know that with God all things are possible!

THE LORD'S PRAYER: SETTING AND BACK-GROUND. Since we are going to explore the details of the Lord's Prayer, it is crucial that we understand its scriptural setting and background. Going through this process will show us the larger message of Jesus in the Gospel of Matthew and how we live out our Christian life as individuals and as a community. Each verse, chapter, and book of the Bible has a specific location and context and needs to be understood in light of its place within the larger Bible. It is very much like looking at an old-fashioned Amish quilt. Amish quilts are usually created from a collection of small colorful patchwork pieces of fabric. I used to live in Lancaster County, Pennsylvania, the capital Amish culture, and every major tourist stop sold classic Amish quilts, the large multi-colored handmade ones that people would use as a bedspread or hang them on a wall for decoration.

If we analyze an Amish quilt, looking at one patch at a time, we can appreciate it for its design, color, and shape. However, when we look at the quilt in a more detailed way, looking particularly at the individual patches that surround that one piece of quilt we see a much larger picture and appreciation for the entire quilt. We may notice that each patch is colored differently or that it has a different pattern or stitching. So too with Scripture. When we read the Lord's Prayer in a larger context, within the context of the Sermon on the Mount, and then in relationship to the entire Gospel of Matthew, and then the rest of the Bible, we will have a much broader and richer understanding of the prayer. One aspect of this book is to help us understand how the Lord's Prayer fits into the rest of the Gospels and the other Scriptures that surround it. After reading this book, you will hopefully have a much better understanding of the scriptural background of the Lord's Prayer which will make it more meaningful for you the next time that you say these very special words.

The Lord's Prayer is located almost in the middle of what we call the Sermon on the Mount, a lengthy sermon delivered by Jesus to His disciples. The Sermon on the Mount is located in the Gospel of Matthew chapters 5–7. Just prior to the Sermon on the Mount, we have Jesus' birth in Bethlehem and His baptism in the Jordan River by John the Baptist, followed by His forty-day temptation in the Judean wilderness. Immediately following the Sermon on the Mount, we have a series of ten miracles done by Jesus followed by the calling of the disciples and then sending them out for ministry. The Sermon on the Mount comes in the very beginning of Jesus' ministry and immediately before a cycle of miracles and further teachings about Christian discipleship. Before reading this book, try to take some time and read the first few chapters of Matthew, especially the Sermon on the Mount, so you can familiarize yourself with the background material that will be included in the following chapters.

After Jesus was tempted by Satan in the wilderness, He left and healed people in the Galilee area, "And He went about all Galilee, teaching in their synagogues and preaching the gospel of the kingdom and healing every disease and every infirmity of the people" (Matthew 4:23). At the end of this chapter, we hear that great crowds of people followed Him from the area around Galilee, Decapolis, Jerusalem, and beyond the Jordan, which is a biblical way of saying people from all of the cities, towns, and villages came out to see Jesus. Jesus certainly was popular in some areas but not in other areas. There are many occasions when the local people did not want Him around, even His own people of Nazareth were not very welcoming, some even wanted to kill Him.

Matthew tells us that Jesus went atop a mountain and sat down and His disciples came to Him. Matthew does not tell us the particular name of the mountain. In the ancient world, mountaintops were places where gods, representing the heavenly or divine realm, encountered humans who were earthly. Mountaintops are places where heaven and earth meet. In Roman and Greek mythology, Mount Olympus was the home of the gods. Tibetans think that the top of Mount Everest is a holy place. In the Old Testament, Moses went to the top of Mount Sinai in order to receive the Ten Commandments. Likewise, Elijah went on the top of a mountain where God spoke to him in a still small voice. Many of these mountains mentioned in the Scriptures were also religious sites and had religious shrines: Mount Nebo, Mount Zion, Mount Tabor, and Mount Hermon, among others.

Jesus begins His sermon with a series of Beatitudes or blessings, "Blessed are the poor in spirit, for theirs is the kingdom of heaven. Blessed are those who mourn, for they shall be comforted" (Matthew

5:1–2). Jesus reverses the old idea that power, profit, authority, and material possessions rule this earth. Rather, Jesus offers His followers another way of looking at life as He preaches about God's Kingdom. Jesus says that those who mourn will be comforted, the meek shall inherit the earth, and that the pure in heart will see God. Jesus presnts us with a reversal of roles, life is not always as it may seem or as it should be. In this world, the rich get richer and the poor keep getting poorer. Yet in the eyes of God, those that have access to wealth and abundance need to share that with the poor. The same sentiment pertains to forgiveness, love, and other spiritual practices. One could easily spend their entire lifetime reading, reflecting, and praying the Beatitudes.

After a long stretch of teaching about Old Testament commandments, Jesus then turns to three important spiritual practices: piety, almsgiving, and prayer:

> Beware of practicing your piety before men in order to be seen by them; for then you will have no reward from your Father who is in heaven. "Thus, when you give alms, sound no trumpet before you, as the hypocrites do in the synagogues and in the streets, that they may be praised by men. Truly, I say to you, they have received their reward. But when you give alms, do not let your left hand know what your right hand is doing, so that your alms may be in secret; and your Father who sees in secret will reward you." And when you pray, you must not

> be like the hypocrites; for they love to stand and pray in the synagogues and at the street corners, that they may be seen by men. Truly, I say to you, they have received their reward. But when you pray, go into your room and shut the door and pray to your Father who is in secret; and your Father who sees in secret will reward you. "And in praying do not heap up empty phrases as the Gentiles do; for they think that they will be heard for their many words. Do not be like them, for your Father knows what you need before you ask Him (Matthew 6:1–8).

This particular Gospel lesson is the one that we hear on Forgiveness Sunday, the Sunday just prior to the beginning of Great Lent. These few verses are very powerful because Jesus warns His disciples how they ought to behave and live. The Old Testament is full of important passages about assisting those in need, especially the poor, widow, and orphan, "Hear this word you cows of Bashan, who are in the mountain of Samaria, who oppress the poor, who crush the needy, who say to their husbands, 'Bring that we may drink'" (Hosea 4:1) and "Woe to those who devise wickedness and work evil upon their beds! When the morning dawns, they perform it, because it is the power of their hand. They covet fields, and seize them; and houses, and take them away; they oppress a man and his house, a man and his inheritance" (Micah 2:1–2). The prophetic words may seem harsh to our modern ear and they are, but they are harsh because the prophets looked around and saw the wickedness and evil in the land and preached a word of repentance.

Ultimately, almsgiving and charity are acts of love which we see in 1 John 4, "Beloved, let us love one another; for love is of God, and he who loves is born of God and knows God" (1 John 4:7). Likewise, one of Jesus' most important teachings is in Matthew 25, where we encounter the parable of the sheep and the goats. The sheep are the ones who performed acts of mercy and charity, for they gave food, drink, clothing, and they visited the sick and the imprisoned. The goats are the ones who neglected to do these things and Matthew concludes these verses by saying, "And they will go away into eternal punishment, but the righteous into eternal life" (Matthew 25:46). The Epistle to James reminds us, "has not God chosen those who are poor in the world to be rich in faith and heirs of the kingdom which He has promised to those who love Him? But you have dishonored the poor man. Is it not the rich who oppress you and drag you into court?" (James 2:5-6). Our commitment to God and to the Kingdom is completely connected and related to our love and service of the neighbor.

After Jesus speaks about fasting and almsgiving, He focuses His attention on prayer. We are reminded that prayer is supposed to be short, not like the Pharisees who heap up lengthy phrases. We hear echoes of other passages in the Gospels where Jesus condemns the Pharisees for practicing their prayer in a self-righteous manner. As with the parable of the Publican and the Pharisee, it was the Publican's very brief and sincere prayer, "God, be merciful to me a sinner" (Luke 18:13) that was acceptable to God rather than the long, very haughty prayer of the Publican. Likewise, in the Psalms, we hear, "The sacrifice acceptable to God is a broken spirit; a broken and contrite heart, O God Thou wilt not despise" (Psalm 51:37). This is King David's prayer after he was chastised by the Prophet Nathan after David sent his friend Uriah off to go into battle so that he could have Uriah's wife Bathsheeba.

Jesus turns from a general comment on prayer to a more specific way as he taught them:

> Our Father who art in heaven,
> Hallowed be thy name.
> Thy kingdom come.
> Thy will be done,
> On earth as it is in heaven.
> Give us this day our daily bread;
> And forgive us our debts,
> As we also have forgiven our debtors;
> And lead us not into temptation,
> But deliver us from evil.

The concluding doxology which we often hear at the end of the prayer, "for Thine is the Kingdom, and the power, and the glory, to the Father, and to the Son, and to the Holy Spirit," is not in the Gospel of Matthew but it is found in the early Christian document called the *Didache*, a first century text which contains teachings of the early Christians. Over time this particular doxology has been incorporated at the end of the Lord's Prayer so that now we often hear it as we conclude reciting or singing the Lord's Prayer.

Moreover, my wish for you as the reader is that we can all try to live according to the Lord's Prayer, which is the real test of our faithfulness to the biblical God. As the epistle to James says, "So faith by itself, if it has no works, is dead" (James 2:17). What we pray with our mouth we must live in our life. In other words our faith in God is an active faith and we need to always keep this in the forefront of our minds. Jesus Himself tells us that faith requires action, "Ask, and it will be given to you; seek, and you will find; knock, and it will be opened to you. For every one who seeks finds, and to him who knocks it will be opened" (Matthew 7:7–8). The words act, see, knock are active words. At the end of the Sermon on the Mount, after Jesus finished teaching His disciples, He told them, "Every one then who hears these words of mine and does them will be like a wise man who built his house upon the rock; and the rain fell, and the floods came, and the winds blew and beat upon the house, but it did not all, because it had been founded on the rock. And every one who hears these words of mine and does not do them will be like a foolish man who built his house upon the sand; and the rain fell, and the floods came, and the winds blew and beat against that house, and it fell; and great was the fall of it" (Matthew 7:24–27). Jesus puts the emphasis not just on the hearing of the teaching but in the doing. Let Jesus' teachings be a warning to us, it is not okay just to hear Jesus' teachings and do nothing. We are called to live and follow these words every day. Our judgment at the end of our life will be based upon putting our complete trust and faith in the one whom loved us from the beginning and who continues to love us even until the end, despite our sinfulness, hard-heartedness, and unrighteousness. The Lord's Prayer is a living, breathing, vibrant prayer that we can all follow during our lifetime.

How to Use This Book. Whether you are reading this book by yourself or in a small group setting, you will need a Bible translation that you feel comfortable reading. There are many different translations available, and it is always good to have several in order to compare the texts. Also take time to look up the many Bible references that are included in the book. You will learn more about the Lord's Prayer, but also you will familiarize yourself with other parts of Scripture.

Some people might also want to use this book in conjunction with journaling, a regular spiritual practice that helps to engage their inner thoughts, temptations, fears, and dreams. A journal is also a record and you can return back to it in the future. In order to help you with small group discussion or in the journaling process, I included a section called "Food for Thought" which will help you better understand the Gospel message. Allow some extra time so that everyone can contribute in the sharing process and that everyone will have ample time to share. Begin and end your session with prayer.

This book is dedicated as a small offering of thanks to my parishioners at the Nativity of the Holy Virgin Orthodox Church in Charlotte, NC, for their continued support, encouragement, prayers, and most importantly, patience! Likewise, I am very grateful for our vibrant adult Christian education program, particularly for our ongoing Bible study. Through regular Bible study we have encountered God speaking to us week after week and have deepened our faith as we read, pray, and study the Word of God. This has also led to our strong support of outreach ministries to the local Charlotte community. We are trying to live out our faith by serving and helping the people around us. I hope that we will have many years together as we all grow in faith, hope, and in love, studying, praying, and living out the Lord's Prayer each and every day.

CHAPTER ONE

OUR FATHER
WHO ART IN HEAVEN

Fathers come in all colors, shapes, and sizes. There are good fathers and unfortunately there are also bad fathers. I had the benefit of having a very good father who was caring and gentle. Donald R. Mills, a.k.a "dad," was not a great thinker or writer, he didn't leave any large legacy behind after he died. He will not be remembered for important acts and his name will never be included in the annals of history. Actually Dad barely graduated high school. He worked at St. Barnabas Hospital in Livingston, NJ, where both he and my mother devoted over twenty-five years of their life. My father was a transporter, bringing patients from their hospital rooms to the Operating Room for surgery, or to the laboratory for medical tests and procedures, or to other places in the hospital. He never said an unkind word about anybody and lived by the maxim, "be more than you show." In other words, don't flaunt yourself, be genuine, be real, be who you are. I always try not to forget that saying. Our family was shocked when dozens of physicians and high-level hospital administrators attended his funeral to pay their last respects. My dad was one of several hundred — hospital employees, yet he apparently touched their life in a deep way since they wanted to say goodbye. I have met many fathers like my father who are good decent people, who work hard to raise a family and be good role models for their children.

In the Scriptures, the biblical God is often referred to as a "Father." Some people think that this term is unique to the New Testament; however, it is mentioned in the Old Testament. One day God called Jeremiah who was only a youth, but God wanted Jeremiah to preach to Israel. Jeremiah thought that he was too young to start a preaching career, but God took hold of Jeremiah and said that he was going to go preach to Israel, "Do not say, 'I am only a youth;' for to all to whom I send you you shall go, and whatever I command you you shall speak. Be not afraid of them, for I am with you to deliver you, says the Lord" (Jeremiah 1:7–8). When God speaks two times, He really means it! So Jeremiah obeyed the Lord and went to Israel and began preaching repentance. At one point God speaks through Jeremiah and says: "I thought how I would set you among My sons, and give you a pleasant land, a heritage most beauteous of all nations. And I thought you would call Me, My Father, and would not turn from following Me. Surely, as a faithless wife leaves her husband, so have you been faithless to Me, O house of Israel, says the Lord" (Jeremiah 3:19–20). These might sound like strong words and they are. God is very angry at Israel for leaving Him and worshipping false idols, as Jeremiah says in the next several verses, "Return O faithless sons, I will heal your faithlessness" (Jeremiah 3:22). So God makes Jeremiah speak harshly to them in order to get Israel to return back to Him. God's relationship with Israel is like that between a father and a son. A father cares for and nurtures his son so that one day he will grow into a fine young man. So too does God do the same with Israel. But the harder God, works the more Israel rebels and runs the other way. This same story is told throughout the Old Testament

Jeremiah's words are also echoed by the Prophet Malachi. We do not know much about Malachi other than his name, which in Hebrew means, "my messenger." Malachi speaks a lot about the Levitical priesthood who was in charge of the rites and rituals of the Jerusalem Temple and like Jeremiah also emphasizes the importance of the covenant in the life of Israel as well, "Have we not all one father? Has not one God created us? Why then are we faithless to one another profaning the covenant of our fathers? Judah has been faithless, and abomination has been committed in Israel and in Jerusalem; for Judah has profaned the sanctuary of the Lord, which he loves and has married the daughter of a foreign god" (Malachi 3:10–11). The Prophet Isaiah also refers to God as father, "For Thou art our Father, though Abraham does not know us, and Israel does not acknowledge us; Thou, O Lord, art our Father, our Redeemer from of old is Thy name" (Isaiah 63:16. See also Psalm 89:27, 1 Chronicles 29:10).

In the beginning books of the Scriptures, what is called the Torah, we encounter the first patriarchs; Abraham, Isaac, and Jacob. These are the "first fathers" of what later became the community of Israel. The word "patriarch" literally means first chief or first father since they were the father of the family, clan, and what eventually became a tribe. Other cultures and societies have paternal or fatherly figures as well. The American Indians had chiefs who were in charge of the well being of the tribe. Germans had the Kaisers and in Russia there were the Tsars. England and France had Kings. These men were the heads of state and leaders of the people. In studying the history of the United States, we often refer to the leaders of the newborn country as the "founding fathers," namely, George Washington, Thomas Jefferson, James Madison, and so forth. These were the first leaders of the thirteen colonies which later became known as the United States of America. In the ancient world, the Roman Emperor was considered to be the father of their people since he offered them prosperity through trade and shipping, public projects through the collection of taxes, and protection through a strong military force.

Jesus refers to the biblical God as His Father, but not just as His personal father, but as "our father," the father of anyone who calls on His name who wants to be his son or daughter in faith. When we call upon God as Father, we become His adopted sons and daughters, His children. Jesus' mission in the world was to make His Father known as we hear in the Gospel of John, "no one has ever seen God; the only Son, who is in the bosom of the Father, He has made Him known" (John 1:18). Later on, in the same Gospel, Jesus says that if you come to know Jesus, you will come to know God the Father. Jesus' main mission is to make His Father known to all nations, peoples, cultures, and languages. Basically, all of Jesus' ministry is to bring the world to know God the Father.

Like all fathers, God sometimes has to discipline His children. I vividly remember my parents disciplining me for doing bad things In the fifth grade, I managed to get into a fist fight on the playground. Needless to say, my parents were not pleased. Then there was the time that I "misplaced" some books in the classroom. When I told my parents, I was disciplined for several days. I could not play outside or watch television. The word discipline is related to the word disciple, a term that pertains to learning. A disciple is a student, someone who learns. Students have to train themselves to study and work hard in order to learn the material. Discipline then is an act of training. Several times throughout the Scriptures, the authors speak about God chastising or correcting Israel. The Prophet Amos makes a list of one condemnation after another, because the nations have broken God's commands and have not been good stewards of what they have been given. After chastising Damascus, Gaza, Tyre, Edom, the Ammonites, Moabites, Juda-hites, finally Amos chastises Israel:

> Thus says the Lord: "For three transgressions of Israel, and for four, I will not revoke the pun-ishment; because they sell the righteous for silver, and the needy for a pair of shoes — they that trample the head of the poor into the dust of the earth, and turn aside the way of the af-flicted; a man and his father go in to the same maiden, so that my holy name is profaned; they lay themselves down beside every altar upon garments taken in pledge; and in the house of their God they drink the wine of those who have been fined."

Amos says that the God of Israel is angry at all these nations for different reasons. Then at the end of this particular passage, the author surprises us by say-ing that God is also very angry towards Israel. Amos saves the harshest condemnation until the end. The book of Amos is short, but the message packs a big punch. Other prophets, such as Hosea, Zechariah, and Ezekiel, have similar condemnations of Israel for their idolatry and unrepentant hearts, for their ne-glect of the widow and orphan, and for the injustice in the world. Yet, as a Father, the biblical God does not give up on His children, whom He loves and cares for very much, so He continues to send the prophets in order to bring Israel back to Him. He chastises Israel in order for them to do His will and to follow Him. He chastises those whom He loves:

> Woe to those who decree iniquities to decrees, and the writers who keep writing oppression, to turn aside the needy from justice and to rob the poor of my people of their right, that widows may be their spoil, and that they may make the fatherless their prey! What will you do on the day of punishment, in the storm which will come from afar? To whom will you flee for help, and where will you leave your wealth? Nothing remains but to crouch among the prisoners or fall among the slain. For all this his anger is not turned away, and his hand is stretched out still (Isaiah 10:1–4).

> Woe to the rebellious children, says the Lord, who carry out a plan, but not Mine; and who make a league, but not of My spirit, that they may add sin to sin; who set out to go down to Egypt, without asking for My counsel, to take refuge in the protection of Pharoah, and to seek shelter in the shadow of Egypt! Therefore shall the protection of Pharoah turn to your shame and the shelter in the shadow of Egypt, to your humiliation. For through his officials are at Zoan and his envoys reach Hanes, everyone comes to shame through a people that cannot profit them, that brings neither help nor profit, but shame and disgrace (Isaiah 30:1–5).

I will recount the steadfast love of the Lord,
the praises of the Lord, according to all that
the Lord has granted us, and the great goodness to the house of Israel which He has granted them according to His mercy, according to
His steadfast love. For He said, surely they are
My people, sons who will not deal falsely; and
He became their Savior. In all their afflictions
He was afflicted, and the angel of His presence
saved them; in His love and in His pity He re-
deemed them; He lifted up and carried them all
the days of old. But they rebelled and grieved
His holy Spirit; therefore He turned to be their
enemy, and Himself fought against them. Then
He remembered the days of old, of Moses His
servant. Where is He who brought up out of
the sea the shepherds of His flock? Where is He
who put in the midst of them His holy Spirit,
who caused His glorious arm to go at the right
hand of Moses, who divided the waters before
them to make or Himself an everlasting name,
who led them through the depths? Like a horse
in the desert, they did not stumble. Like cattle
that go down into the valley, the Spirit of the
Lord gave them rest. So Thou didst lead Thy
people, to make for Thyself a glorious name
(Isaiah 63:10–14).

Israel turned away from God, and God disciplined them in order to bring them to repentance.
Whether you are reading the Prophet Isaiah, Amos,
Hosea, or Ezekiel, you will hear similar passages
since the prophetic word is a primarily a word of re-

pentance, that Israel as a community has lost her way and God the Father is going to bring her back because He loves them very much. These are words of discipline because God loves His people just as most fathers love their children. God wants us to worship Him, to love Him, and to serve Him. Actually, the entire Bible, including the prophets and the Torah, all can be reduced to one axiom or commandment, to love God with all of our heart, soul, strength, and mind and our neighbor as ourself. By calling on God as our Father, we begin on this path of love.

FOOD FOR THOUGHT

1. Each of us has a different type of relationship with their earthly father. Some of us have a very strong relationship, while others may have a distant or strained relationship. Take some time and reflect on your relationship with your father. How would you describe this relationship? Is it good, bad, or indifferent?

2. In what practical ways can you improve your relationship with your father? Do you talk with him on a regular basis? Do you still ask his advice? Is he a part of your life?

3. We can all become more gentle and loving if we do not focus so much on peoples' faults, foibles, warts, and wrinkles, but on their good parts. As we read in the Book of Genesis, God created everything good, and everyone has both good and bad character traits mixed together. This, of course, also pertains to our fathers. This week try to focus on the good qualities in your father. You may choose to share your thoughts with him.

4. The Scriptures tell us that love and forgiveness cover up a multitude of sins and are the ingredients to wholeness and holiness. Try to forgive your father if he has wronged you in any way. If you hold any anger or resentment against him, let it go now. Life is too short to be angry.

CHAPTER TWO

HALLOWED BE THY NAME

Many words in the Bible may seem strange to us today, words like "justification," "righteousness," and "immortality." We don't read about justification too often in the daily newspaper or hear about righteousness on the evening news. When was the last time you used justification in a conversation with a friend? Many personal names in the Bible are also very strange to our ears: Methusalah, Abithar, and Nebuchednezzar among others. One doesn't often hear people named Shadrach, Mesach, or Abednego these days! Yet these names were once popular a long time ago. I guess that if Moses or Abraham were alive today, they would think that Johnny, Susie, and Billy are strange names as well.

Our personal names were given to us at birth. My parents named me William Christopher Mills after my deceased uncle William who died in World War II. Uncle William, or Bill as they called him, was my father's eldest brother and was already a young adult when my father was born. My parents also liked the name Christopher but they couldn't decide which order to put them so they decided on William as my first name and then Christopher as my middle name. William is a German name that means "the conqueror," and Christopher is a Greek name that means "the carrier or bearer of Christ." I have always been fascinated by the etymology of names and how names have developed and changed through the centuries. One can spend a lifetime studying names and their meanings. Names also identify us from other people and make us unique and distinct from other people.

The biblical God has more than one name. Actually, He has a lot of names. We usually refer to Him as Father, but He also goes by the name the Mighty One, the Lord of Hosts, the Redeemer, and simply, the Lord. If you have some time, it might be a good practice to look up some of God's other names. You can find them in a Bible dictionary or concordance. One of His earliest names that we come across in the Bible is Yahweh, which is sometimes translated as Jehovah. Yahweh means "the one who is" or the "living one" and was the name that He told Moses on Mount Sinai. Moses wanted to tell the Israelites the name of God, and he asked God what they should call Him. So God told him that His name is Yahweh. Yahweh sounds sort of funny to our ear, but in the ancient world it was funny too. What type of God is called "I am who I am"? Basically, God told Moses that He is beyond our control. In the ancient world, if you knew the name of a god or deity, you could control them. However, the biblical God is different. He didn't want to be controlled, so He told Moses to call Him Yahweh.

The Bible also tells us that God's name is very special. It was so special that the Jews could not pronounce His name but for only once per year by the High Priest in the Jerusalem Temple who uttered God's name in the Holy of Holies. When the Jews read from the Torah, they did not pronounce God's name as it is spelled out as Yahweh, but rather they said Adonai, which is Hebrew for Lord, as in the phrase "my Lord." God's name is so holy that the Jews were forbidden to pronounce it.

The Lord's Prayer reminds us that God's name is supposed to be "hallowed," which is a fancy word for holy. The word holy means special or set apart. We use this word holy a lot in Church as in, "Holy God, Holy Mighty, Holy Immortal have mercy on us," which comes from Isaiah, chapter 6. Isaiah has a vision of God's throne and all the angels who are encircling the throne and crying out, "Holy, holy, holy, Lord of Sabbaoth, heaven and earth are filled with Thy glory." Then an angel of the Lord comes and touches Isaiah's lips with a burning charcoal and his response is that he is a sinful man living with a sinful people. When Isaiah is in the presence of God, he realizes that he is sinful and unclean.

We also hear a lot about God's holiness in the New Testament. When the Apostle Paul addresses the Christian Churches, he refers to them as saints, which means holy, as we see in 1 Corinthians 1:2, "To the Church of God which is at Corinth, to those sanctified in Christ Jesus, called to be saints together with all of those in every place call on the name of the Lord Jesus Christ, both their Lord and ours." This is also echoed in the Letter to the Hebrews 3:1, "Therefore, holy brethren, who share in a heavenly call, consider Jesus, the apostle and high priest of our confession" and in 1 Peter 1:15, "As obedient children, do not be conformed to the passions of your former ignorance, but as he who called you is holy, be holy yourselves in all your conduct, since it is written, "You shall be holy, for I am holy," and finally, in 2 Timothy 1:9, "Do not be ashamed then of testifying to our Lord, nor of me His prisoner, but share in suffering for the Gospel in the power of God, who saved us and called us with a holy calling, not in virtue of our works but in virtue of his own purpose." Paul wants to reassure his flock that they are holy because they are now a part of God's larger family and are called to be holy as God is holy.

God's name is very interesting because in the Old Testament world there were many different gods which had very strange names: Gog, Magog, Molech, Baal, and Beelzebub. Each of these gods had statues as well as temples and sacrifices. They had their own sacrificial system, complete with burnt offerings.

People would often go to the temple of a local god or goddess and burn incense or make a burnt offering of an animal or a grain. The priest would keep some of the offering for themselves as a type of payment and then give back the rest to the person who offered it. There are many examples of the Israelites worshipping gods and idols. When Moses was on Mount Sinai receiving the Ten Commandments, his brother Aaron was making a golden calf from the gold bracelets and jewelry from the Israelites. The Israelites were tired of waiting for Moses and wanted to worship something, so they created a golden calf to worship.

Yahweh, as He is known, is the God of the patriarchs and of the prophets and of our savior Jesus Christ. We pray then in the Lord's Prayer that God's name is always holy and that in His name we can find our salvation and our hope.

FOOD FOR THOUGHT

1. Everyone is unique in the eyes of God, as the Psalmist says even the hairs of our head are numbered. Take some time to reflect on the sanctity of life, on the life of those around you, and the sanctity of the whole world.

2. What does it mean that God wants us to be holy, just as holy as He is? The Apostle Paul refers to his communities as being "holy" or as we also say "saints." How can we become saints in this world? How can we better live the Christian life and faith in the culture and society? How can we become beacons of light, love, peace, and justice?

3. What are some of the ways that we can help people live a holy life? How can we help them be better Christians?

CHAPTER THREE

THY KINGDOM COME

My daughters love bedtime because bedtime means books! Just before they go to bed, my wife and I read them stories, and most often they are stories about princes and princesses, of kings and castles, and knights in shining armor. Of course, there are also yucky witches, warlocks, and wizards too, which make for great reading. When reading these stories, you quickly realize that every prince has a big castle with a village, armed soldiers, trumpets blowing, and beautiful princesses in fancy dresses. Each story, of course, also includes a kingdom.

The Bible also speaks a lot about kingdoms. In the Old Testament, we hear about the kingdom of Israel and Judah, as well as the kingdom of Samaria, Assyria, and Babylon. We hear about the Hittites and Amorites, the Moabites and the Jesubites, who seem to always be fighting one another. When reading Scripture, we read a lot about kingdoms and warfare.

We often forget that Jesus was born and raised in a very important kingdom, which was the Roman Empire. The Roman Empire was very large and spanned a great distance, including modern day Italy, Greece, Turkey, most of the Middle East, North Africa, and that northern Europe and England, which they called Britannia.

At the time of Jesus' birth, Caesar Augustus was the emperor. Augustus, who was formerly known as Octavius, was the adopted son of the great emperor Julius Caesar. The Gospel of Luke tells us this much in the opening chapters, "In those days a decree went out from Caesar Augustus that all the world should be enrolled. This was the first enrollment, when Quirinius was governor of Syria" (Luke 2:1–2). Luke wants to show us that Jesus was born under important rulers in a strong empire. Under Augustus, the Roman Empire had a long-lasting peace called the *Pax Romana*. Augustus was a very strong and powerful ruler and established a very strong military and army. During his reign, many public roads, public buildings, and ports were built and constructed. This was a very prosperous time in Roman history.

The Roman Empire was controlled by a very large military and navy which protected the Empire but also maintained peace and concord. The Empire also had a strong legal system and rules and regulations for collecting taxes and, of course, entertainment. The famous Circus Maximus in Rome hosted gladiator games as well as horse races. Every Roman city had at least one circus as well as a hippodrome, a horse racing stadium. People who lived in the ancient world were very aware that they were living in a very real kingdom full of power, control, wealth, and religion.

In the Gospels, Jesus often refers to a kingdom too, but it is not the Roman Empire to which He refers, but rather to the kingdom of Heaven. Sometimes He uses the phrase kingdom of God, but they are synonymous. Jesus used very common images and symbols in order to speak about the new kingdom. This kingdom must not have been very easy to understand because Jesus went to great lengths to explain it and used many images and metaphors to get His point across to His disciples. Surely when Jesus mentioned the Kingdom of Heaven, people must have immediately thought about the Roman Empire because that was the only visible and viable kingdom around. They saw the sheer power and authority of Rome in daily life. The coins they used were inscribed with the Emperor's portrait. If they went into large cities, they would have encountered the Roman military. They would have used roads constructed by Roman slaves and used ports built by the Roman military. When they went to market, they had to use the Roman system of weights and measures. Everyday life was impacted by the fact that they were living in the Roman Empire.

Yet, when Jesus was speaking of His Father's kingdom, He was not talking about bricks and mortar building projects, military operations, roads or ports, money and tax revenue, He was talking about something all together different. In order to explain what He meant, Jesus used parables or little short stories. However, these parables are not just one-dimensional and do not describe the entire message, but rather, different aspects of it. He used common symbols or parables to explain this kingdom. Many of these stories appear in the Gospel of Matthew:

> Another parable He put before them, saying, "The kingdom of heaven is like a grain of mustard seed which a man took and sowed in his field; it is the smallest of all seeds, but when it has grown it is the greatest of shrubs and becomes a tree, so that the birds of the air come and make nests in its branches." He told them another parable. "The kingdom of heaven is like leaven which a woman too and hid in three measures of flour, till it was all leavened."

> "For the kingdom of heaven is like a householder who went out early in the morning to hire laborers for his vineyard. After agreeing with the laborers for a denarius a day, he sent them into his vineyard. And going out about the third hour he saw others standing idle in the market place; and to them he said, 'You go into the vineyard too, and whatever is right I will give you.' So they went. Going out again about the sixth hour and the ninth hour, he did the same. And about the eleventh hour he went out and found others standing; and he said to them, 'Why do you stand here idle all day?'

They said to him, 'Because no one has hired us.' He said to them, 'You go into the vineyard too.' And when evening came, the owner of the vineyard said to his steward, 'Call the laborers and pay them their wages, beginning with the last, up to the first.' And when those hired about the eleventh hour came, each of them received a denarius. Now when the first came, they thought they would receive more; but each of them also received a denarius. And on receiving it they grumbled at the householder, saying, 'These last worked only one hour, and you have made them equal to us who have borne the burden of the day and the scorching heat.' But he replied to one of them, 'Friend, I am doing you no wrong; did you not agree with me for a denarius? Take what belongs to you, and go; I choose to give to this last as I give to you. Am I not allowed to do what I choose with what belongs to me? Or do you begrudge my generosity?' So the last will be first, and the first last."

In the first series of sayings, Jesus compares the Kingdom of Heaven to a mustard seed. Mustard seeds are the smallest of the herbs that we use; we use ground up mustard seed to make mustard and to use it for hot dogs and hamburgers. It grows up and is like a very big bush. However, in Palestine, mustard is very common, it grows everywhere, very much like kudzu that we have in the southeast, a very durable, strong, and pesky weed that is very difficult to get out of the garden. If we pull it out it returns again. If we try to kill it, some will survive and will grow back. In other words, we can try to contain and control kudzu, but it never seems to budge. Well, Jesus tells us that the kingdom is like a mustard seed, it grows where it will and is durable and even pesky at times. In other words, it is out of immediate control; it has a life of its own.

Similarly Jesus uses the image of a woman putting some yeast in three measures of flour. If you have ever made bread, you know exactly what Jesus is trying to say. When making bread, you use the smallest amount of yeast, usually one or two teaspoons per batch. You add the yeast and some sugar into a warm bowl of water and let it rise, then you add flour, much more flower than yeast. And this flour bubbles up higher and higher. When you put the dough in the oven, it grows. I usually make three or four loaves of bread, and it only takes about one tablespoon of yeast to make the dough rise. It is so hard to believe that this small amount of yeast makes that much dough rise but it does. Moreover, you really do not see the yeast work, it happens almost invisibly.

What do these two parables teach us about the Kingdom? Well, perhaps they teach us that even small almost insignificant things, like mustard seeds and yeast, are actually very potent and work right under our eyes but we don't always seem to notice them working Growing plants take time and grow at a snail's pace. Likewise, like plants, yeast multiplies and grows by leaps and bounds. Perhaps they teach us that the kingdom cannot be controlled or contained, it has a mind of its own, growing and working where it wants to work. Ultimately we do not control the Kingdom, God does. Our job is not to get in God's way!

There are many more examples about the kingdom of heaven. Jesus uses the parable of the wedding banquet as well as the parable of the ten virgins each one describing a different aspect of the kingdom. The wedding banquet reminds us that even those who are invited can find excuses not to come to the wedding feast. However, the king was not satisfied so he invited other people from far away, from the highways and byways which means that God will invite other people to His Kingdom. This parable also shows us that people have the freedom to accept or reject God's invitation. The parable of the ten virgins reminds us to be extra vigilant because we are not sure when the Lord will return again to judge His creation. Once He arrives it is too late, the five virgins who trimmed their lamps gained entrance while the other five virgins were left outside.

When we pray "Thy kingdom come," we pray that God's kingdom come now, that we can live and work in this world and identify with the kingdom of heaven in the "here and now." When we are living the life of the Spirit, which Paul speaks about in his letter to the Galatians, love, joy, peace, kindness, and self-control, we are living according to the kingdom.

When we are giving sacrificially of our time, talent, and treasure, we are living according to the kingdom. When we are practicing forgiveness and living a life of repentance, we are living according to the kingdom. In other words, while Jesus has not yet returned to judge the world in all His glory we can still live as if we were already in the Kingdom, which is not a bad thing at all. Actually, it is exactly what Jesus intended as He told His disciples that the kingdom of heaven is among or within you.

And we also have to ask ourselves, who is the head of this Kingdom? The answer, of course, is God, as we see in Psalm 93:

> The Lord reigns; He is robed in majesty;
> The Lord is robed He is girded with strength
> Yea, the world is established; it shall never
> be moved;
> Thy throne is established from of old;
> Thou art from everlasting
> The floods have lifted up O Lord,
> The floods have lifted up their voice
> The floods lift up their roaring.
> Mightier than the thunders of many waters
> Mightier than the waves of the sea,
> The Lord on high is mighty!
> Thy decrees are very sure;
> Holiness befits thy house,
> O Lord forevermore

Similar Psalms refer to God's kingly activity in the world as the Psalmist David describes God's power and strength, "For the Lord is a great God, and a great King above all gods" (Psalm 95:3); "Sing praises to our King, sing praises! For God is the king of all the earth; sing praises with a Psalm! (Psalm 47:7); "O sing to the Lord a new song, for He has done marvelous things! His right hand and His holy arm have gotten Him victory" (Psalm 98:1); and "The Lord reigns; let the peoples tremble! He sits enthroned upon the cherubim; let the earth quake!" (Psalm 99:1). God's power extends over all the earth, not just over Israel but as we see in the prophetic writings, He is also the God over all the nations, Assyrians, Babylonians, Hittites, and Amorites. All peoples, cultures, and nations are under God's care and authority. We may not understand how all of this works, but the Scriptures say that God's kingdom is established for all nations if they choose to believe in Him as king and as God.

Likewise, Jesus Himself is identified with God's kingly power. Several times in the New Testament we encounter Jesus kingly activity; He heals the sick, raises the dead, walks on water, and speaks with the authority of God. Just as Jesus was beginning His earthly ministry, He meets Nathaniel, Andrew, and Philip, and Nathaniel exclaims, "Rabbi, You are the Son of God! You are the King of Israel" (John 1:49). When Jesus was born, the wise men from the East came to pay homage to the Christ child and they inquired of King Herod, "Where is he who has been born King of the Jews?" (Matthew 2:2). Later, at the end of Jesus' life as He is going to His crucifixion, Pontius Pilate inquired of Jesus, "Are you the King of the Jews?" (Matthew 27:11).

So when we pray that may God's kingdom come, we pray that His kingdom comes now and that we live as if we were already in the kingdom. Jesus is the one who brought His Father's Kingdom, and this is a great gift. This means that we must live out our faith each and every day. Faith is not just for our heads, something that we believe, but also for our hearts and the hands. We must think about our faith, believe in this faith, and then respond to this faith. Faith requires action.

A big part of the Christian life is living according to what is set forth in the Lord's Prayer. We reduce faith as only attending church services. Faith is an action, God calls and we respond. We respond out of our trust and hope in God's promise to us. In turn we share this faith with other people. We are called to respond to the needs of others as we saw in the Beatitudes. We can become the light, leaven, and salt in this world. We can share our faith with others by being the hands and feet of Christ in this world. Jesus Himself tells His disciples that even when they give a cup of water in His name, they are doing a great deed. There is such a great need for goodness, truth, justice, and material assistance in the world. There are so many people in this world who are hungry, helpless, and hopeless, those who need our assistance. We cannot turn them away. God sends us to help them. We will not solve all of the world's problems overnight; we cannot prevent homelessness or poverty; we cannot prevent all acts of war and violence. However, one thing is certain: If we are Christian disciples, we must live out this faith with those people around us, making the world a better place to live, serving the poor and the needy, comforting the sick and the distressed. We can live and die knowing that we did not solve all of the world's problems, but we did try to make this world more humane and peaceful.

FOOD FOR THOUGHT

1. The Scriptures tell us that there are two kingdoms, the kingdom of this world where profit, power, and materialism reigns and then there is the kingdom of God where peace, love, justice, and beauty reign. We literally have one foot in each kingdom since we are always battling between the earthly and heavenly kingdom. How can you live more in God's kingdom and practice the fruits of the kingdom (peace, love, justice) today? How can you help others live in this Kingdom?

2. We all have a duty to help one another in our spiritual journey. We are called to support and care for one another. This week, try to make a conscientious effort to be a positive influence on someone in your congregation, family, or workplace. How can you be the "yeast" or the "light" to people around you?

3. We pray in church about the union of all, about peace, and about love. When you leave church on Sunday, think about how you can become an ambassador of unity, peace, and love around you. How can you personally make this world a better place for the next generation? How can you be a better Christian example to your family, fellow parishioners, and fellow citizens?

CHAPTER FOUR

THY WILL BE DONE ON EARTH AS IT IS IN HEAVEN

I often hear people inquire, "What is God's will for me," as if God has a different will for each of us. Sometimes I think that we have reduced the Christian faith to a type of exaggerated individualism as in: What can God do for me? How can God improve my life? How can the Church make me a better person? However, the Bible is not about what can God do for me personally. God is always interested in His community. God always has a community of persons whom He cares about. Church is not about individuals per se, but about a community of persons whom come to know and to love God. This does not mean that God does not love each one of us as individual persons, but that we are people within a larger community of faith.

We all have our unique situations in life, some of us are married, others are single, some have children, others are childless, some of us are rich, others are poor. Some are highly educated, some have a remedial or very basic education. Some are ordained priests and others are laymen. Despite our differences in life, we all are called to love God with all our heart, soul, mind, and strength and to love our neighbor, a basic teaching found in both the Old and New Testaments. When people asked Jesus what is the greatest commandment, He quotes from the book of Deuteronomy. That everything in the Law and the Prophets can be reduced to that one teaching: love God and neighbor. We see this, of course, in other passages in Scripture, 1 John 4, "Beloved, let us love one another; for love is of God, and he who loves is born of God and knows God. He who does not love does not know God; or God is love. In this the love of God was made manifest among us, that God sent His only Son into the world, so that we might live through him" (verses 7–9). Later on in the same chapter, John continues along the same lines, "If anyone says, 'I love God,' and hates his brother, he is a liar; for he who does not love his brother whom he has seen, cannot love God whom he was not seen. And this commandment we have from Him, that he who loves God should love his brother also" (1 John 4:20–21).

But loving our neighbors is not always that easy. You may have a neighbor who plays loud music into the early hours of the night. Or you might have neighbors like the ones that we had when our family moved to Charlotte, NC. Several young men lived in the second floor apartment above us. He and his friends would sit on the outside porch and smoke cigarettes and unknowingly drop ashes on us down below who were enjoying the outdoors. The only consolation was that their spare change also fell from their pockets so we overlooked their toxic habits, using their spare change for our laundry! Neighbors do come in all sorts of sizes, shapes, colors, and temperaments, and sometimes they are not easy to live with.

We usually do not choose our neighbors. If you move into an established neighborhood, you will already have neighbors. College students usually get assigned roommates by the student life department. Clergy do not get to choose their parishioners, and teachers do not choose their students. Most often we just receive whomever the Lord sends our way. Sometimes the Lord sends some "interesting" people my way, but I try to love them the best that I can. Our family has been very lucky to have friendly neighbors wherever we lived. By good I mean neighbors who genuinely cared for one another. If one of us went on vacation, they would look out for our house. If one of us didn't see an elderly neighbor for a while, they would call over just to make sure everything was okay. It is good to live in places where people care for one another, a blessing from God.

In the New Testament, the classic teaching of the love of the neighbor is best expressed in Jesus' parable of the Good Samaritan. Jesus says that a man was traveling from Jerusalem to Jericho and fell among robbers. The narrow and rocky road from Jerusalem to Jericho was nearly 20 miles that went form 2,500 feet above sea level in Jerusalem to about 770 feet above sea level in Jericho, which is a very deep descent on treacherous paths. Jericho was one of the popular cities in the Old Testament; it was in Jericho where Joshua blew his horn and the walls of the city came tumbling down. Jericho was also in the vicinities of the tribes of Benjamin and Joseph, two important tribes in the Old Testament. Furthermore, in the New Testament, Jericho is where Jesus heals Bartimaeus and later visits Zachaeus who also lives in Jericho (Matthew 20:29 and Luke 19:1).

The parable says that three different people walked by the man on the side of the road, a priest and a Levite followed finally by a Samaritan. The priests and Levites were members of the religious elite in Judaism and hailed from the priestly lineage of Aaron. Luke does not tell us the exact reasons why both the priest and the Levite passed by the man alongside the road, but we can infer that since the man was bloody that they refused to have contact with him. It was against the Law to come into contact with anyone who was either unclean or if there was blood involved.

The third person who came by that way was a Samaritan. This small fact might not sound too important today, but during the time of Jesus, the Samaritans were considered religious and social outcasts. The Samaritans were a mixed race of Jews and pagans and lived in the area called Samaria and were considered outcasts according to the Jews. Samaritans are mentioned at several intervals in the Scriptures; we have the famous story of Jesus and the Samaritan woman in the Gospel of John who was living in adultery as mentioned in John 4. Also in the book of Acts one of the first miracles took place with a Samaritan. To a first century audience, this lesson would have been an impossibility, no Samaritan would have taken the time to help a stranger who was clearly unclean.

Details are very important in literature. Even the smallest detail helps the reader understand the flow of the story. The Bible is no different in this regard. Luke tells us some very important details. First and foremost is that Samaritan used his own financial resources to help the hurt man, using his own oil and wine to help cauterize the wounds and then put him on his beast and brought him to an inn. In antiquity, oil and wine were not only used for food but also for medicinal purposes. Oil was a balm that helped soothe sores and wine was used as an antiseptic and it was used as a cleansing agent as we hear in the Book of Psalms, "and wine to gladden the heart of man and oil to make his face shine and bread to strengthen man's heart" (Psalm 104:15. See also Deuteronomy 28:40). In the New Testament, we have evidence of this in the epistle to James, "Is anyone among you suffering? Let him pray. Is any cheerful? Let him sing praise. Is any among you sick? Let him call the elders of the church, and let them pray over him anointing him with oil in the name of our Lord; and the prayer of the faith will save the sick man, and the Lord will raise him up; and if he has committed sins, they will be forgiven. Therefore, confess your sins to one another, and pray for one another, that you may be healed" (James 5:13–15).

Just when we think the story is over, it continues. Not only did the Samaritan take this hurt man to the inn, but he took time out of his own trip, at least an entire day plus an evening. He also used his own money, which we are told was about two days wages. Two days' wages back then might not seem like much, but two days' wages are still two days' wages. If you are making $20.00 per hour, two days' wages would be about $320.00, which even today is a lot of money.

We are reminded that we are called to do the same for other people as well. Jesus tells us that the entire Law and the Prophets can be reduced to one commandment, love of God and neighbor, "Hear, O Israel: the Lord our God is one Lord; and you shall love the Lord your God with all your heart, and with all your soul, and with all your might" (Deuteronomy 6:5). We fulfill one commandment by fulfilling the other, but both are needed in this life.

If God's will for us is to love and care for our neighbor then how do we actually go about doing this? Well, it really depends on the specific situation in which we find ourselves. There are so many ways to show love and care for someone else. If there is a parishioner or friend that you know who is sick maybe you can go visit them, send them a card, or call them. You can collect canned food for the hungry or used clothing for the homeless. You can collect spare change during Advent or Lent and donate that money to a local charity. You can volunteer at a local soup kitchen or women's shelter. There are countless ways to help other people. The main thing is that we respond to people's need in a way that is meaningful and according to the Gospel.

FOOD FOR THOUGHT

1. We pray that the Lord's will be done in our life. Yet very often things get in between us and God. Make a list of the things that are preventing you from following the Lord. How can you overcome these things? Remember, there is always room for improvement!

2. When we pray the Lord's Prayer, we usually think of it in individual terms, but also we pray this prayer with a community, usually a parish community. Similarly to the question above, what are some of the things in your parish that are preventing the community from following the Lord fully and completely? How can you help other people in your faith community be better Christians? How can your local parish do God's will in your area? How can you take the love of the neighbor to the "next level" and reach out and help other people around you?

CHAPTER FIVE

GIVE US THIS DAY OUR DAILY BREAD

Bread is one of the most basic staples in life and it comes in many shapes and sizes: bagels, baguettes, challah, croissants, pita, rye, sourdough, pumpernickel, whole wheat, or just plain good old fashioned white bread. Bread can be big, small, medium, long, or short. It can have a hard crust or a soft crust. No matter what shape or form, bread always tastes good! There is nothing better than coming home on a cold winter's day to the smell of freshly baked bread. Just the thought of it makes my mouth water. Whether you like your bread with regular butter or with peanut butter and jelly, bread is always delicious. It goes great with a hot cup of coffee or tea. I am amazed that something so simple as flour, water, yeast, and sometimes an egg or two, mixed together and baked in the oven can produce something so delicious.

Bread is mentioned quite often in the Scriptures too. In the book of Exodus, God instructs Moses to

get ready because He is planning to deliver them
from the hand of Pharoah. The Israelites did not
have time to let their bread rise because they had
to take it with them on their long trip. So they took
their belongings, including their unleavened bread,
and followed Moses across the Red Sea. They left so
quickly they had very little to eat. Thankfully God
always has a plan. He told Moses that He was going
to send them bread from heaven, which was called
manna. The Bible says that manna looked like white
frost on the ground. They were told to collect the
manna every day but to take a double portion on
Friday because on Saturday, which was the Sabbath,
was a day of rest and no work could be done. Whatever it was, they didn't like the manna too much
since the Israelites started to grumble against God,
they were looking for something else to eat. They
surely must have eaten a lot of bread during all those
years in the wilderness.

However, in the Bible, bread does not only refer
to physical bread, it is also mentioned in conjunction
with God's teaching. In the book of Deuteronomy,
God tells Israel the following, "That man does not
live by bread alone, but that man lives by everything
that proceeds out of the mouth of the Lord" (Deuteronomy 8:3). Later, in the New Testament, Jesus
quotes this exact same verse as He rebukes the Devil
when He is tempted three times in the wilderness.
The entire passage from Deuteronomy is here below:

"All the commandment which I command you this day you shall be careful to do, that you may live and multiply, and go in and possess the land which the Lord swore to give to your fathers. And you shall remember all the way which the Lord your God has led you these forty years in the wilderness, that He might humble you, testing you to know what was in your heart, whether you would keep His commandments, or not. And He humbled you and let you hunger and fed you with manna, which you did not know, nor did your fathers know; that He might make you know that man does not live by bread alone, but that man lives by everything that proceeds out of the mouth of the Lord … So you shall keep the commandments of the Lord your God, by walking in his ways and by fearing Him" (Deuteronomy 8:1–10).

The rest of the book of Deuteronomy continues in the same vein and the words "commandments," "ordinances," and "statues" are repeated several times throughout the chapter. These words refer to God's word or God's Law which was given to Israel at Sinai. In other words, just as God fed Israel the manna from heaven, so too He fed them with His words and teachings, which are both lifegiving. The Sinai event was not a one-time deal but was an action that needed to be remembered for every generation. The biblical God is a God who speaks and His Word gives life.

This theme is also seen in the book of Ezekiel. Ezekiel is sent to preach to the Israelites who are in captivity in Babylon. Jerusalem is in ruins and Israel has been captured and carried off to exile. God tells Ezekiel:

> "But you, son of man, hear what I say to you; be not rebellious like that rebellious; open your mouth, and eat what I give you." And when I looked, behold, a hand was stretched out to me, and, lo, a written scroll was in it; and He spread it before me; and it had writing on the front and on the back, and there were written on it words of lamentation and mourning and woe. And He said to me, "Son of man, eat what is offered to you; eat this scroll, and go, speak to the house of Israel." So I opened my mouth, and He gave me the scroll to eat. And He said to me, "Son of man, eat this scroll that I give you and fill your stomach with it." Then I ate it; and it was in my mouth as sweet as honey (Ezekiel 2:8–3:3).

Here Ezekiel is given the scroll to eat which is the Word of God and it is "as sweet as honey." However, the words that come out of Ezekiel's mouth are not sweet at all, they are phrases of "mourning and woe" against Israel which is described as a "rebellious house" and who have "stubborn heads," words that appear throughout the book of Ezekiel. God is very angry at Israel because they turned away from Him so He sends Ezekiel to Israel as a warning that their attitude must change.

Furthermore, in Psalm 119, which is also the longest Psalm in the Bible, we have a meditation or reflection on God's word or Law. Nearly all of the

176 verses contain the words, ordinances, laws, testimonies, or statutes. Here the Psalmist reflects on the beauty and perfection of God's word, for the Word is the food that nourishes His people every day. Below is just a sampling of some of the many verses in Psalm 119 which reflect the deep love of God's teachings:

> Remember Thy word to Thy servant,
> in which Thou hast made me hope.
> This is my comfort in my affliction that
> Thy promise gives me life.
> Godless men utterly deride me,
> but I do not turn away from Thy law.
> When I think of Thy ordinances from of old,
> I take comfort, O Lord.
> Hot indignation seizes me because of the wicked,
> who forsake Thy law.
> Thy statutes have been my songs in the house of
> my pilgrimage.
> I remember Thy name in the night, O Lord,
> and keep Thy law.
> This blessing has fallen to me,
> I have kept Thy precepts.
> The Lord is my portion;
> I promise to keep Thy words.
> I entreat Thy favor with all my heart
> be gracious to me according to Thy promise.
> When I think of Thy ways,
> I turn my feet to Thy testimonies
>
> Oh, how I love Thy law!
> It is my meditation all the day.
> Thy commandment makes me wiser than my

enemies, for it is ever with me.
I have more understanding than all my teachers
for Thy testimonies are my meditation.
I understand more than the aged, for I keep
Thy precepts.
I hold back my feet from every evil way, in order
to keep Thy word.
I do not turn aside from thy ordinances, for Thou
hast taught me.
How sweet are Thy words to my taste, sweeter than
honey to my mouth!
Through Thy precepts I get understanding;
therefore I hate every false way.
Thy word is a lamp to my feet and a light to
my path.

You might want to take some time and read the entire Psalm, taking time to reflect on the various descriptions, metaphors, symbols, and images that are associated with God's Word.

One of the clearest examples of this in the New Testament is found in John chapter 6, where we have a series of three events. First we encounter the feeding of the five thousand, a miracle contained in all four Gospels. The crowds have been following Jesus for a long time and are very hungry. Jesus takes five loaves and two fish and multiplies them for the people. There was so much bread left over that the disciples gathered twelve baskets, which represents fullness and completion. Twelve is an important number in the Bible, we have twelve tribes of Israel, twelve disciples, and then here the twelve baskets of left over bread. Then immediately after this miracle, Jesus walks on the water. It is night and the disciples are on a boat in the middle of the Sea of Tiberias, which is another name for the Sea of Galilee. There was a strong wind and the boat was tossing to and fro. Then they thought they saw a ghost, but it was Jesus coming to them on the water. Finally, we have a long dialogue with Jesus and the Pharisees who are the Jewish leaders. At one point in this long discussion, Jesus exclaims publicly:

> Jesus said to them, "I am the bread of life; he who comes to Me shall not hunger, and he who believes in Me shall never thirst. But I said to you that you have seen Me and yet do not believe. All that the Father gives Me will come to Me; and him who comes to Me I will not cast out. For I have come down from heaven, not to do My own will, but the will of Him who sent Me; and this is the will of Him who sent Me, that I should lose nothing of all that He has given Me, but raise it up at the last day. For this is the will of My Father, that everyone who sees the Son and believes in Him should have eternal life; and I will raise him up at the last day." The Jews then murmured at Him, because He said, "I am the bread which came down from heaven." They said, "Is not this Jesus, the son of Joseph, whose father and mother we know? How does He now say, 'I have come down from heaven'?" Jesus answered them, "Do not

murmur among yourselves. No one can come to Me unless the Father who sent Me draws him; and I will raise him up at the last day. It is written in the prophets, 'And they shall all be taught by God.' Everyone who has heard and learned from the Father comes to Me. Not that anyone has seen the Father except Him who is from God; He has seen the Father. Truly, truly, I say to you, he who believes has eternal life. I am the bread of life. Your fathers ate the manna in the wilderness, and they died. This is the bread which comes down from heaven, that a man may eat of it and not die. I am the living bread which came down from heaven; if anyone eats of this bread, he will live for ever; and the bread which I shall give for the life of the world is My flesh."

Jesus refers to Himself as the bread of life, the bread from heaven, and then the living bread. Jesus is superior to the manna that was given to them in the wilderness, He is the bread of heaven and the bread that lives. Every time Jesus speaks, the crowds seem to get angrier and angrier, "The Jews then murmured at Him, because He said, 'I am the bread which came down from heaven'" (John 6:41). The word "murmur" is the same word that is used in Exodus when God gave the Israelites manna from heaven and after several days of eating the same food they murmured at God. The word murmur literally means that they yelled or rebuked God. Jesus is the bread of life.

However, Jesus is not talking about bagels or Wonder bread, but about His teaching.

So, on the one hand, when we pray in the Lord's Prayer "give us this day our daily bread," we are petitioning God to give us the teaching and a word that will sustain us each and every day. This teaching is from God Himself who sits on His throne in heaven and who gave Moses the Ten Commandments. The teaching gives life because it is from God Himself. The Gospels are words, but these words give us life, they feed and nourish us. The Apostle Paul reminds his co-worker Timothy of this as he writes:

> Command and teach these things. Let no one despise your youth, but set the believers an example in speech and conduct, in love, in faith and purity. Till I come, attend to the preaching and teaching. Do not neglect the gift that you have, which was given you by prophetic utterance when the council of elders laid their hands upon you. Practice these duties, devote yourself to them, so that all may see your progress. Take heed to yourself and to your teaching; hold to that, for by so doing you will save both yourself and your hearers (1 Timothy 4:11–16).

Jesus' teaching is a word of hope in this world, that no matter what trials and tribulations we encounter, no matter how far we all in life, God is still God and He is the beginning and the end, the Alpha and the Omega, who is ultimately the judge over all creation. His words give us life in a world of death and darkness. Our pastors and bishops have a particularly important ministry as they are specifically called to preach and teach the Christian faith through their sermons, Bible studies, bulletins, adult education programs, and other venues. Pastors are supposed to be highly educated and continually reading, studying, and praying the Scriptures. When pastors are being fed and nourished with the Word of God, they are then able to provide this food for their parish community. Hopefully his teachings will feed you too on our way to the Kingdom. When the entire Church is living according to God's Word, then everyone is being encouraged, inspired, and edified. When we learn and pray the Scriptures, we are growing closer to one another, bringing the community of faith together. Take the time to read, study, and pray the Scriptures, you will be fed and nourished for the rest of your life.

FOOD FOR THOUGHT

1. Many people have asked me how they can get more out of my sermons. I always tell them to read the Sunday Epistle and Gospel readings before coming to church. Pay attention during the sermon itself, making mental notes of a word, idea, or concept that you find interesting or inspiring. Talk about the sermon with your family in the car ride home after church, perhaps your spouse or children heard something that you did not hear.

2. Many Christians have DBS — Dusty Bible Syndrome! We have Bibles but do not read them. If we are reading, praying, and studying the Word of God on a daily basis, we will be better prepared to serve as His disciples. If we do not know what a disciple is supposed to do, how can we be one? So start today and begin reading the Bible. It is better to start slowly, reading a few verses at a time, perhaps even an entire chapter each day. Join a Bible study at Church or perhaps one in your local neighborhood or at work. You don't know, you might even learn something!

3. There are many resources available for Bible study. Some of these resources are included in the back of this book. Take some time and learn more about Scripture and spiritual formation. In addition to Bible study, parishes may also sponsor book clubs, perhaps your book club could study

and share *Our Father* or another book included
in the Bibliography. When we are learning, the
Body of Christ will grow and flourish.

CHAPTER SIX

AND FORGIVE US OUR DEBTS AS WE HAVE FORGIVEN OUR DEBTORS

Every time I open the newspaper these days I read about debt. Whether it is our national debt that continues to increase or the growing personal debt of the millions of Americans, it seems as if everyone is in some financial debt; home mortgages, credit cards, student loans, personal loans, or car loans. Basically, Americans owe a lot of money. Now with our national home mortgage crisis that is sweeping across America, we see that home foreclosures are on the rise and people are being forced into personal bankruptcy. Others are loosing their jobs due to a reduction in staff. Things do not look pretty these days.

A monetary debt is money that we owe to a person or an institution. Thankfully our family has two major debts, a home mortgage and a student loan from college. When we pay off our mortgage and the student loan, we will be debt free. A few years ago we paid off our car loan. It was a small loan but nonetheless it was a debt that we wanted to pay off. It felt so good to write that last check to the car loan company. We now own both of our cars debt free!

Monetary debt and the forgiveness of this debt is a major theme in the Book of Leviticus, specifically the Sabbatical Year and the Jubilee Year. For six years, farmers and herdsman could work the land, plant and harvest crops, and raise cattle. However, in the seventh year the land was to remain fallow and not tilled, worked, or harvested, as a remembrance of God's saving them from Pharoah, "In the seventh year there shall be a Sabbath of solemn rest for the land, a sabbath to the Lord; you shall not sow your field or prune your vineyard. What grows of itself you shall not reap, and the grapes of your undressed vine you shall not gather" (Leviticus 25:4-5). In many ways, the Sabbatical year was like an extended Sabbath day, a lengthy time of rest. For an entire year, the Israelites were forbidden to work their land. After the seventh Sabbatical Year, which would be a period of forty nine years, there was a Jubilee Year, a phrase that from the Hebrew word "yohel," which means ram's horn since a ram's horn was blown proclaiming the Jubilee. In the Jubilee Year, all leases on the land expired and people returned back to their ancestral estates, "Then you shall send abroad the loud trumpet on the tenth day of the seventh month; on the day of atonement you shall send abroad the trumpet throughout your land. And you shall hallow the fiftieth year, and proclaim liberty throughout the land to all its inhabitants; it shall be a jubilee for you, when each of you shall return to his property and each of you shall return to his family" (Leviticus 25:10–12). The Jubilee Year was a time for forgiveness of personal and business debt. The Jewish spiritual tradition maintains the ritual of blowing a ram's horn at the feast of Rosh Hashanna, the Jewish New Year. At the beginning of the New Year, the Jews ask forgiveness of one another, forgiving the many spiritual debts that they owe other people or that other's owe to them.

Scholars are not sure if the Israelites actually followed the Jubilee Year; it seems very extraordinary, that they would not till or work the land for an entire year. People need to work the land to survive. However, the rationale behind this command is that the people must remember that the land is not theirs that their financial obligations to others have to be reconciled because this is what God expects from us. This notion of forgiving financial debt is taken up and expressed in the Lord's Prayer as Jesus speaks about our need to forgive others what they owe to us. The Jubilee years are the background for the forgiveness of debts in the Lord's Prayer.

The Lord's Prayer invites us to ask God to forgive our debts, just as we have already forgiven our debtors, those people who owe us. So if my neighbor promises to pay back the small loan that I gave him that means that he is indebted to me. The prayer assumes that we have already forgiven or are already in the process of forgiving other people. However, in the Lord's Prayer Jesus is not speaking about money. We are required to forgive people the things that they owe us, usually things like kindness, love, care, or concern. Maybe someone is holding a grudge against us or is jealous. Jesus often taught about forgiveness, as we see in the scriptural passages below:

> For if you forgive men their trespasses, your heavenly Father also will forgive you; but if you do not forgive men their trespasses, neither will your Father forgive your trespasses.

> If your brother sins against you, go and tell him his fault, between you and him alone. If he listens to you, you have gained your brother. But if he does not listen, take one or two others along with you, that every word may be confirmed by the evidence of two or three witnesses. If he refuses to listen to them, tell it to the church; and if he refuses to listen even to the church, let him be to you as a Gentile and a tax collector. Truly, I say to you, whatever you bind on earth shall be bound in heaven, and whatever you loose on earth shall be loosed in heaven. Again I say to you, if two of you agree on earth about anything they ask, it will be done for them by My Father in heaven. For where two or three are gathered in My name, there am I in the midst of them." Then Peter came up and said to him, "Lord, how often shall my brother sin against me, and I forgive him? As many as seven times?" Jesus

said to him, "I do not say to you seven times, but seventy times seven.

"Therefore the kingdom of heaven may be compared to a king who wished to settle accounts with his servants. When he began the reckoning, one was brought to him who owed him ten thousand talents; and as he could not pay, his lord ordered him to be sold, with his wife and children and all that he had, and payment to be made. So the servant fell on his knees, imploring him, 'Lord, have patience with me, and I will pay you everything.' And out of pity for him the lord of that servant released him and forgave him the debt. But that same servant, as he went out, came upon one of his fellow servants who owed him a hundred denarii; and seizing him by the throat he said, 'Pay what you owe.' So his fellow servant fell down and besought him, 'Have patience with me, and I will pay you.' He refused and went and put him in prison till he should pay the debt. When his fellow servants saw what had taken place, they were greatly distressed, and they went and reported to their lord all that had taken place. Then his lord summoned him and said to him, 'You wicked servant! I forgave you all that debt because you besought me; and should not you have had mercy on your fellow servant, as I had mercy on you?' And in anger his lord delivered him to the jailers, till he should pay all his debt. So also my heavenly Father will do to every one of you, if you do not forgive your brother from your heart."

According to these three passages, and there
are others that are very similar, forgiveness is an es-
sential part of the Christian life. Forgiveness is not
optional, but mandatory. Jesus does not say, "if you
forgive" but "when you forgive." God's forgiveness is
dependant on our forgiveness of the debts of other
people, which really is a big deal if you think about
the many ways that people hurt us and cause us pain.
The third Scripture selection above about the forgiving king shows this very clearly. Just as the king forgave his servant the great debt, the servant should
have forgiven his friend even the little debt that he
owed. The parable ends on a sour note, "You wicked
servant! I forgave you all that debt because you besought me; and should not you have had mercy on
your fellow servant, as I had mercy on you?' And in
anger his lord delivered him to the jailers, until he
should pay all his debt. So also my heavenly Father
will do to every one of you, if you do not forgive your
brother from your heart." The servant was originally
forgiven his small debt to the king but yet when his
slave couldn't pay him he wasn't as merciful as the
king was merciful to him.

Probably one of the most memorable parables in
the New Testament is the parable of the Prodigal Son,
which is sometimes referred to as the parable of the
Forgiving Father which is found in the Gospel of Luke
15:11–32. Luke tells us that a man had two sons and
the younger son requested that he might receive his

inheritance before his father died. This might seem like a normal request; however, in the ancient world, the eldest son inherited everything.

So then the younger son takes his inheritance and goes off into a far country and squanders his inheritance in "loose living." He also found himself in hunger and want since a famine arose in that country. This boy was so hungry that he had to live off of the same food that the pigs ate. The Old Testament declares that anything with cloven feet, such as pigs, are unclean so this man was living in utter poverty and uncleanness.

The young boy wanted to return back home. Rather, the father immediately told his servants to prepare a celebration for his son. The story doesn't end there. All the while, the eldest son who never left the father was upset that the father was making such a big celebration for his other son. In other words, he was jealous that the father never game him a party. The father responded to the son by saying, "Son, you are always with me, and all that is mine is yours. It was fitting to make merry and be glad, for this your brother was dead, and is alive; he was lost, and is found" (Luke 15:31–32). Just as the father in this story forgave and welcomed back his son, so too, does the Lord welcome us back as well. However, forgiveness also means that there is a specific action or event that needs to be forgiven and reconciled, there is no such thing as a general forgiveness. People cause harm to other people all of the time and these are concrete action or deeds. In other words, we have specific and concrete examples of sinful actions and behaviors.

Forgiveness is a theme woven throughout the Bible. However, forgiveness doesn't stand alone, it goes together with repentance. Repentance means to turn around, to literally change one's direction. We can use the analogy of driving a car. If you are going from point A to point B and somewhere along the road you realize you are driving in the wrong direction, you turn around and re-orient yourself, trying to find your way again. Repentance means to turn away from sin, from all of the things that block our path from following Christ and doing His will; anger, jealousy, lack of love, despair, and lack of faith. The list is endless. Practicing forgiveness is only part of the equation, but this must go hand in hand with repentance. The Gospel actually begins with repentance as we hear in the preaching of John the Baptist, "Repent for the Kingdom of heaven is near."

The Old Testament prophets forewarned Israel of their living in sin and their need for repentance and change. The prophets looked around and saw the wealthy causing economic problems for the poor, the raging of wars, and many injustices and illegal activities. The prophets preached a word of repentance to the people so that the people would eventually return back to the Lord. It was not up to the prophets if Israel changed, their duty was to continue to preach and let the Word of God do its work:

Is not this the fast that I choose; to loose the bonds of the wickedness, to undo the thongs of the yoke, to let the oppressed go free, and to break every yoke? It is not to share your bread with the hungry, and to bring the homeless poor into your house; when you see the naked, to cover him, and not to hide yourself from your own flesh? Then shall your light break forth like the dawn, and your healing shall spring up speedily; your righteousness shall go before you, the glory of the Lord shall be your rear guard. Then you shall call, and the Lord will answer; you shall cry, and He will say, Here I am (Isaiah 58:6–9).

Woe to those who devise wickedness and work evil upon their beds! When the morning dawns, they perform it, because it is in the power of their hand. They covet fields and seize them; and houses, and take them away; they oppress a man and his house, a man and his inheritance. Therefore thus says the Lord; Behold, against this family I am devising evil, from which you cannot remove your necks; and you shall not walk haughtily, for it will be an evil time. In that day they shall take up a taunt song against you, and wail with bitter lamentation, and say, "We are utterly ruined; he changes the portion of my people; how he removes it from me! Among our captors he divides our fields" (Micah 2:1-4).

Woe to her that is rebellious and defiled, the oppressing city! She listens to no voice, she accepts no correction. She does not trust in the

Lord, she does not draw near to God. Her officials within her are roaring lions; her judges are evening wolves that leave nothing till the morning. Her prophets are wanton, faithless men; her priests profane what is sacred, they do violence to the law. The Lord within her is righteous, he does no wrong; every morning he shows forth his justice, each dawn he does not fail; but the unjust knows no shame (Zephaniah 3:1–5).

These are just three of many passages that deal with this theme of sinfulness and repentance. In general, this theme is taken up by all the prophets in one form or another. Of all the Christian practices, forgiveness and repentance seem to be the most difficult to practice. How do you forgive someone who treats you badly? Some of us have experienced tragic events in life, perhaps suffered emotional or physical abuse, or been the brunt end of racist or sexist remarks. Yet despite all of this, we are still called to forgive.

The Gospel reminds us that God is an all-loving Father and has forgiven all of our sins on the cross of His Son. Jesus is the Lamb of God who takes away the sins of the world, and He takes my sin and your sin on Himself and crucifies it on the cross. If Jesus has done this for us, shouldn't we at least try to forgive others, even a tiny bit? Jesus never said that turning the other cheek was easy. Nor did Jesus say that praying for ones' enemies was any easier either. I know that I struggle with this all the time, but I think we need to at least make an effort, and try to forgive those who have caused us harm. The alternative option is to remain bitter and angry for the rest of our lives.

The Church has given us the Sacrament of Holy Confession to help us in the process of repentance. I always feel much better after confession, telling the priest all of my sins, the actions or inactions that have caused others' grief. Then he offers me a few words of encouragement, showing me how to get back on the right path, and then I leave. It feels like a big rock was lifted from my back. We carry these sins around with us and they really are like heavy burdens, always there constantly reminding us of our fallen humanity. I hope that you will feel the same way about confession. If you have trouble going to confession or if you do not know what to say to your priest, go to him after Church and ask to speak with him about how you can better prepare yourself for confession.

FOOD FOR THOUGHT

1. The Sacrament of Confession or Reconciliation
    is a powerful spiritual practice that helps us deal
    with our family secrets, scandals, and pain. It is
    quite comforting to confess one's sins to a priest
    and be able to get some spiritual insight and di-
    rection afterwards. We generally go to confession
    during Advent and Great Lent; however, you are
    more than welcome to come at other times of the
    year. Don't neglect this very important part of
    our spiritual tradition, it is very helpful.

2. The word "sin" in Greek means to "miss the mark,"
    as if we are shooting an arrow into a bullseye and
    the arrow misses, it is considered off the mark.
    Sins are not only things that we do wrong such
    as lie, steal, or cheat, but also includes things that
    we should do but we don't, like being more lov-
    ing, forgiving others, being more generous with
    our time, talents, and treasure. Take a few mo-
    ments and make a list of your sins and things
    that you have done to offend someone else in
    your life. After looking at this list, how do you
    feel? Are there ways to make amends for your
    sins? Do you always ask forgiveness from people
    whom you have offended?

3. The author of the epistle to the Hebrews says that
    love covers up a multitude of sins. The more we
    show love and become love to one another we
    cover up our sins. Take a few moments and think

how you can be more loving this week to the people around you. How can you make their life a little easier? How can you express love each and every day?

CHAPTER SEVEN

AND LEAD US NOT INTO TEMPTATION BUT DELIVER US FROM THE EVIL ONE

This last phrase in the Lord's Prayer seems strange. It is strange asking God not to lead us into temptation because why would the biblical God, the God who gave us His Word, who sent the prophets, and who gave us His Son, want to tempt us? Well, the answer is He is not tempting us at all. The actual phrase can also be rendered, "save us from the day of trial" or in other translations it means "test," as in if we take a test or a final examination at school.

When Jesus was praying in the garden of Gethsamene, He was very worried; He was fully aware that He would have to endure the inevitable, betrayal and eventually death which He previously predicted three times in the Gospel. Jesus goes into the garden with Peter, James, and John and asks them to sit and watch with Him:

> And Jesus began to be greatly distressed and troubled. And He said to them, "My soul is very sorrowful, even to death; remain here, and

watch." And going a little farther, He fell on the ground and prayed that, if it were possible, the hour might pass from Him. And He said, "Abba, Father, all things are possible to Thee; remove this cup from Me; yet not what I will, but what Thou wilt." And He came and found them sleeping, and He said to Peter, "Simon are you asleep? Could you not watch one hour? Watch and pray that you may not enter into temptation; the spirit is willing, but the flesh is week." And again He went away and prayed, saying the same words. And again He came and found them sleeping, for their eyes were very heavy; and they did not know what to answer Him. And He came the third time, and said to them, "Are you still sleeping and taking your rest? It is enough; the hour has come; the Son of man is betrayed into the hands of sinners. Rise, let us be going; see, My betrayer is at hand" (Mark 14:32–43).

For Jesus, His "trial" was this ultimate test of faith, to put His complete and utter trust in God or to walk away, denounce God, and be saved. Mark tells us that in Gethsamene Jesus chose the first option and accepted God's will and was arrested, put on trial and then crucified. We pray that we do not have to endure this difficult decision and have our faith tested in this way. We ask God to save us from this because it really is too difficult, as we hear in the writings of the Apostle Paul, "No temptation has overtaken you that is not common to man. God is faithful, and He will not let you be tempted beyond your strength, but with the temptation will also provide the way of escape, that you may be able to endure it" (I Corinthians 10:13), as well as in Hebrews, "For we have not a high priest who is unable to sympathize with our weaknesses, but one who in every respect has been tempted as we are, yet without sin" (Hebrews 4:15).

Just as Jesus was tested in the garden of Gethsemene, so too was Israel was tested in the Old Testament, "And you shall remember all the way which the Lord your God has led you these forty years in the wilderness, that He might humble you, testing you to know what was in your heart, whether you would keep His commandments or not" (Deuteronomy 8:2).

Furthermore, we ask God to deliver us from evil or from the evil one. It is clear when we look around this world, there is a lot of evil: drugs, war, terrorism, racism, sexism, theft, adultery, extortion, and murder. Both good and evil are portrayed in our cultural icons as well: Batman fighting the Joker, Luke Skywalker fighting Darth Vader, Superman fighting Lex Luther. Books, movies, and plays reveal the ongoing battle between good and evil, light and darkness, truth and deception. It always makes a good story line and entertaining television. Evil in movies and in literature is not an abstraction, but it is very real. Many people suffer terrible injustices in this world. Soldiers who experience warfare are often traumatized by the blood and guts of bullets and bombs. They return home paralyzed or with amputated limbs. Wives are physically and emotionally abused by husbands. Children are abandoned. People suffer hunger due to unjust governments. People are addicted to drugs or alcohol. Every day we read about more and more evil in this world and it is very real.

In Scripture, evil is personified in the person of the devil or Satan. Satan has been popularly portrayed as a man with a red suit, horned ears, and a pitch fork. However, in Scripture, we do not have a picture of the devil; he is called the deceiver, the one who deceives and is full of lies. He is also called the accuser and acts like a prosecutor accusing the victim in front of the judge who is God the Father as we see in the passage from the Prophet Zechariah, "Then he showed me Joshua the high priest standing before the angel of the Lord, and Satan standing at his right hand to accuse him. And the Lord said to Satan, 'the Lord rebuke you, O Satan! The Lord who has chosen Jerusalem rebuke you!'" (Joshua 1:1–3).

Satan appears at various places in Scripture, but has some prominence in the book of Job:

> Now there was a day when the sons of God came to present themselves before the Lord, and Satan also came among them. The Lord said to Satan, "Whence have you come?" Satan answered the Lord, "From going to and fro on the earth, and from walking up and down on it." And the Lord said to Satan, "Have you considered My servant Job, that there is none like him on the earth, a blameless and upright man,

who fears God and turns away from evil?" Then Satan answered the Lord, "Does Job fear God for nought? Hast Thou not put a hedge about him and his house and all that he has, on every side? Thou hast blessed the work of his hands, and his possessions have increased in the land. But put forth Thy hand now, and touch all that he has, and he will curse thee to Thy face." And the Lord said to Satan, "Behold, all that he has is in your power; only upon himself do not put forth your hand." So Satan went forth from the presence of the Lord (Job 1:6–12).

Here in the beginning of the book of Job, as well as elsewhere in Job, Satan is allowed to tempt Job but not kill him, and he is always under God's control. Satan appears numerous times throughout the book of Job, afflicting Job with sores on his body, taking away his home, children, farm, and lands. Eventually Job's wife leaves him. Job is all by himself, sitting in sackcloth and ashes. Yet even with Satan testing Job's faith, he never backed down and rejected God.

Furthermore, in the New Testament, the devil appears immediately after Jesus' baptism and tempts Jesus three times in the wilderness, each time with material or earthly temptations, trying to get Jesus to reject God and the commandments:

Then Jesus was led up by the Spirit into the wilderness to be tempted by the devil. And He fasted forty days and forty nights, and afterward He was hungry. And the tempter came and said to Him, "If you are the Son of God, command these stones to become loaves of bread." But He answered, "It is written, 'Man shall not live by bread alone, but by every word that proceeds from the mouth of God.'" Then the devil took Him to the holy city, and set Him on the pinnacle of the temple, and said to Him, "If you are the Son of God, throw yourself down; for it is written, 'He will give His angels charge of you, and on their hands they will bear you up, lest you strike your foot against a stone.'" Jesus said to Him, "Again it is written, 'You shall not tempt the Lord your God.'" Again, the devil took Him to a very high mountain, and showed Him all the kingdoms of the world and the glory of them; and he said to Him, "All these I will give You, if You will fall down and worship me." Then Jesus said to him, "Be, Satan! for it is written, 'You shall worship the Lord your God and Him only shall you serve.'" Then the devil left Him, and behold, angels came and ministered to Him (Matthew 4:1–11. See also Mark 1:12–13; Luke 4:1–13, Hebrews 2:18; 4:15).

Jesus endured being tempted by food, by self-destruction by taking His own life, and then with the power and glory of the riches of this world. Three times Jesus rebukes Satan. The Gospel of Luke recounts the same series of events; however, Luke concludes his passage in the following manner, "and when the devil had ended every temptation, he departed from Him until an opportune time" (Luke 4:12–13). So in the Lord's Prayer, we pray that God delivers us from any temptation of the evil one and that our faith may not be tested as Jesus was tested. As our Lord and Savior Jesus has made a pathway to the Kingdom and He has accomplished all things for us.

FOOD FOR THOUGHT

1. Jesus was tempted three times in the desert with food, earthly power, and with material possessions. Each of us has our particular temptations. Take some time and reflect on the particular material or spiritual temptations that bother you. How can you try to overcome these temptations? How can you be more aware of your life and the impact that you have on other people?

2. You might not realize it, but sometimes we can be temptations to other people. We can actually help other people sin if we participate with them in gossip, slander, laziness, and so forth. Think about how you can be a good role model and be a beam of light in the life of your family and friends rather than be a stumbling block to your friends and family.

BIBLIOGRAPHY

Bianchi, Enzo. *Praying the Word: An Introduction to Lectio Divina*. Kalamazoo, MI: Cistercian Publications, 1998.

_____. *Words of the Inner Life* Toronto: Novalis, 2002.

Brown-Taylor, Barbara. *An Altar in the World: A Geography of Faith*. San Francisco: Harper Collins, 2009.

Johnson, Luke Timothy. *Living Jesus: Learning the Heart of the Gospel*. San Fransisco, CA: Harper Collins, 1999.

Martin, James. *Becoming Who You Are*. Mahwah, NJ: Hidden Spring Books, 2006.

Norris, Kathleen. *Amazing Grace: A Vocabulary of Faith*. NY: Riverhead, 1998.

Schmemann, Alexander *Our Father* (trans.) Alexis Vinogradov. Crestwood, NY: St. Vladimir's

Seminary Press, 2002.

Stevenson, Kenneth. *The Lord's Prayer: A Text in Tradition*. Minneapolis, MN: Augsburg Fortress Pres, 2004.

Williams, Rowan. *Where God Happens: Discovering Christ in One Another*. Boston, MA: New Seeds, 2005.

Wright, N. T. *Lord and His Prayer*. Grand Rapids, MI: William Eerdmans, 1997.

ABOUT THE AUTHOR

Fr. William Mills, Ph.D., is the rector of the Nativity of the Holy Virgin Orthodox Church in Charlotte, NC. Fr. Mills received his Bachelor of History from Millersville University of Pennsylvania and then pursued theological studies at Saint Vladimir's Orthodox Theological Seminary in Crestwood, NY, where he received his Master of Divinity and Master of Theology degrees. He then pursued advanced theological studies at the Union Institute and University in Cincinnati, Ohio, where he received his doctorate in Pastoral Theology. Fr. Mills is the author of several commentaries on the Gospel readings of the liturgical year, including *Feasts of Faith: Reflections on the Major Feast Days* (Rollinsford, NH: Orthodox Research Institute, 2008). Fr. Mills is available for parish and clergy retreats. Visit his personal website at www.williamcmills.com.